Kati –

Adopt
Don't
Shop !

Please
rescue !

Peggy Rydberg
ΣΡΥ
PC #4
♡

ADOPTED LIKE ME

BY:

PEGGY A. RYDBERG
For: Mom and Dad

Cover illustration by Adrienne Ricci-Cox.

**Author photograph used by permission,
taken by Mark Stanley**

Published April 2015

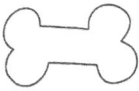

In loving memory of
Sadie and Jazz – my beloved
Yorkies who inspired me
to write this story.

Special thanks to:
Kristin Hiller, Lynn Mandelbaum,
Sheryl Nolan, Anna Soderlund
and Kelsie Wright
And a very special thank you to my
friend and editor, Michelle Volgenau.

CHAPTER 1

"BUZZ, BUZZ, BUZZ," sounded her alarm clock. Olivia slowly opened her eyes, stretched and hit the snooze button. She turned over on her side in hopes of getting a few more winks before she had to get out of bed. But just as she was snug and cozy, her Dad shouted from the kitchen, "breakfast will be ready in ten minutes!" Olivia could smell pancakes and warm maple syrup, which were her absolute favorites.

"Michael, Olivia, come get it while it's hot!" Olivia was by no means a morning person, but she suddenly got a whiff of the bacon that was sizzling in the frying pan. She quickly threw on her clothes and ran down the long spiral staircase. She even beat her brother to the table, which was very unusual.

"Good morning Dad. Did you put chocolate chips in the pancakes the way I like them?" "I sure did," said Dad. She placed a huge pat of butter in the center of her stack and then dowsed them with lots of warm maple syrup. "Please pass the bacon, Mike." The bacon was nice and crispy, just the way she liked it.

"I guess Mom has already left for work," said Olivia. "Yes, she had another early morning meeting in Atlanta, and was out of the house by 5:30," said Dad. Olivia took a final sip of her orange juice and then ran upstairs to get her backpack. She combed her messy hair and brushed her teeth. Michael followed right behind.

"You two are going to miss the bus if you don't get a wiggle on," called Dad. They came barreling down the stairs and Dad greeted them each with a brown paper sack lunch that he had prepared the night before. Olivia and Michael grabbed their jackets from the coat hook and then hugged their Dad good-bye.

As Olivia was going out the front door, she mumbled to herself, "I wish Mom could be here in the mornings to see us off to school." She was not sure if her father heard her or not, but she didn't really care one way or the other.

CHAPTER 2

It was a beautiful, sunny spring morning, as Olivia and her brother walked to the bus stop. This was Olivia's favorite time of the year. She took a deep breath and could smell the fragrant flowers in the air. The daffodils, tulips, and irises were in full bloom. The birds were singing happy little songs and were pleased that the weather was warming up.

Olivia was skipping over the cracks on the sidewalk, a little game she liked to play each morning, while Michael had his head buried in a book. They were about halfway to the bus stop when Olivia heard a little whimpering sound. As she continued to skip, the sound became louder. And, when the whimpers were almost too loud to ignore, she turned to see what was there.

She couldn't believe her eyes. Under a dogwood tree, nestled in a pile of pine straw, were two of the most adorable puppies. She knelt down to get a closer look. They were crying and shaking.

"Where is your mother?" she asked the poor little pups.

By this time, Michael was way ahead of her and almost to the bus stop and screamed for her to hurry up. She couldn't force herself to leave these helpless little creatures. They would surely get hit by a car and they were cold and hungry. She took off her light pink hooded sweatshirt and carefully wrapped the tiny pups in it.

She quickly caught up to her brother and showed him her newly found treasures. "Where did they come from?" he asked. She pointed over to the tree where she had found them.

"Well, what are you going to do with them?" Michael asked.

"I am going to take them to school with me, silly," replied Olivia.

"Don't get them too close to me. You know how allergic I am to animal fur."

Olivia knew only too well. She had longed for a furry pet of her own and was always begging her parents for one. They currently had a gold fish named Sammy. "Whoop-tee-do! What can you do with a fish? You can't play with it or take it for a walk. All you can do is stare at him and watch him swim around in his bowl," she would tell her parents over and over again. But that was always the end of the discussion. Case closed.

CHAPTER 3

Olivia carefully placed the puppies in her backpack, still wrapped in her pink sweatshirt. She didn't want the bus driver to see them or she would surely turn them in once they got to school. She made sure the flap on her backpack was nice and loose so that the puppies would get plenty of air.

When the bus arrived, she walked as fast as she could to the very back and took an empty seat. She tried to act as natural as possible in hopes of not attracting any attention to her wiggling backpack.

She took out her lunch and began to feed the pups her peanut butter and jelly sandwich. They were so hungry that they devoured it in no time at all. She gave them each a hug and a kiss on the tops of their heads, and told them that everything was going to be okay.

As Olivia entered her fourth grade classroom, she quickly walked past Ms. Wright. She softly whispered to the puppies that they must be very quiet. She sat down at her seat and placed the pups in her desk. She was sure that they were about a pound each, and therefore fit very comfortably.

The next task at hand was to get them some water. She unscrewed the top of her thermos and filled it with cold water from the sink in the back of the classroom. She placed the cup in her desk and the puppies, not understanding what was going on, began to walk in the water. They were splashing around in it as if it were a baby pool. Even though Olivia was a bit mad that her books were now soaked, she couldn't help but chuckle at the sight of the puppies having so much fun.

With their bellies full and having played in the water, they were now ready to settle down for a nap. She tucked them into her sweatshirt and told them to have sweet puppy dreams.

CHAPTER 4

"Good Morning class," said Ms. Wright in her always cheery voice. "Please take your seats and turn in your math book to page 128. Today we will be learning how to add simple fractions."

The morning seemed to drag on forever, but it was finally lunch time. Up until now, the puppies had been fast asleep and had been no trouble at all. As the class lined up to go to the cafeteria, the puppies started playing and growling at each other. Then suddenly, one of them let out a faint bark. Olivia started coughing loudly to cover up the sound.

Madeline, who was her very best friend in the entire universe, and also happened to sit right next to her, heard the bark and asked her what was going on. "You promise not to tell anyone?" asked Olivia.

"I promise," said Madeline.

"Pinky swear?"

"Pinky swear," she repeated.

Meanwhile, the rest of the class had filed out into the hallway and were on their way to the cafeteria. Madeline and Olivia lagged behind.

"Well, what's going on?" asked Madeline.

"OK, OK," said Olivia and she pointed to her desk where the puppies were wrestling with one another.

"Oh my gosh! They are so adorable," said Madeline.

The puppies were jet black with some reddish-brown markings on their paws, muzzles, and the tips of their ears. Their coats were silky smooth and they had the cutest little black button noses. Their tails were short and stubby. One pup had ears pointed up and the other had them pointed down.

"What kind of puppies are they?" asked Madeline.

"I have no idea," said Olivia. "All I know is that they are sweet and they need my help."

The girls each picked up a puppy and they peaked out the classroom door to make sure no one was coming. They looked to the left, then to the right and the coast was clear.

"Where are we going?" whispered Madeline.

"We have to take the puppies outside for a potty break!" Olivia whispered back.

There were a lot of children playing outside for recess. They quickly ducked behind a large bush and put the puppies on the ground. Just then a little boy walked past them and noticed the puppies. Before he had a chance to speak, Olivia said, "do you like my battery operated puppies?"

Kindergarteners are so gullible, they will believe just about anything you tell them, she thought to herself. "Wow, they look so real," said the little boy. And off he went to play on the swings with his friends.

"Phew, that was a close one," said Madeline.

"We better hurry up and get to the cafeteria before someone notices that we aren't there," said Olivia. So the two girls and the two puppies headed to the cafeteria.

CHAPTER 5

The pups were safely nestled in the pouch of Olivia's sweatshirt. Madeline walked in front of her to conceal the bulge in Olivia's stomach. The two girls sat with their class and began eating as fast as they could. Their lunch period was almost over and they were both starved. Madeline shared her ham and cheese sandwich, since Olivia had given her peanut butter and jelly sandwich to the pups that morning.

Ms. Wright came over and told the class to line up. But when Olivia stood up, she noticed that the puppies were gone. Her heart sank and she began to panic. When she finally caught a glimpse of them, it was too late. A second grader had tripped over one of the pups and she and her tray of spaghetti and meatballs crashed to the floor.

The students clapped and cheered and some even screamed. There was total chaos in the cafeteria until in came "The Warden." It was actually the school principal, Mrs. Clark, but she was so strict that the students nicknamed her "The Warden." She flicked the lights off and on to get everyone's attention.

"Who is responsible for these hairy beasts?" said Mrs. Clark, in the sternest voice imaginable. Olivia scooped up the puppies, stepped forward and said in a very quiet voice, "I am, Mrs. Clark."

"In my office now! And bring those creatures with you!" barked The Warden. "The rest of you go back to your lunch and let's get some order in here." All Madeline could do was go back with the class and wait and wonder what would happen to her best friend and those darling little puppies.

CHAPTER 6

Olivia was no stranger to the principal's office. She had been sent there on several occasions. She wasn't a bad kid, really. Trouble just seemed to find her.

"Have a seat," said Mrs. Clark in a stern voice. Olivia was trembling, but tried not to let her see she was scared. She had a reputation of being tough and she wasn't about to change that now. "It is no big deal, I was simply minding my own business on the way to the bus stop, when I came across these tiny little puppies. I couldn't very well leave them there," explained Olivia.

"You know that we do not allow animals in school. You broke the rules and will have to be punished. I am calling your parents and asking them to come and pick you up immediately. You are suspended from school for the remainder of the day. You leave me no choice but to call animal control to come and get these dogs."

Olivia begged her not to call animal control. She felt like crying, but maintained her cool image. "They might put them to sleep if someone doesn't claim them!" exclaimed Olivia.

"That is none of my concern. I am only interested in the safety and well-being of my students," replied Mrs. Clark in a harsh tone. She had about as much compassion and personality as a big pile of garbage, thought Olivia.

"That is all. You are dismissed. Wait in the front office for your parents to come and get you." Her face was stern and unforgiving.

She knew it would be her Dad that would pick her up. He stayed at home and was in charge of the household and the kids. Mom was a high-powered attorney in downtown Atlanta and could rarely leave the office. Her father was going to be so disappointed in her.

..."yes Mrs. Clark. I understand. I will be there as quickly as I can. And again, I do apologize for the trouble my daughter has caused." Olivia overheard her Dad saying to The Warden on the phone.

Olivia waited on a hard plastic chair for her Dad. She was nervously tapping her foot and twirling a strand of her long blond hair around her index finger. Her beautiful aqua blue eyes could not look anywhere but at the off-white tiled floor. She was a very petite girl, actually the smallest kid in the fourth grade. It didn't seem to bother her and maybe that is why she portrayed herself as being a tough girl. She rarely showed her emotions and would never let anyone see her cry.

CHAPTER 7

As Olivia's Dad, George, drove to school, he reflected back to the day that he and his wife Cindy flew to Russia to adopt their precious bundle of joy. She was just three months old and living in horrible conditions in a very run down orphanage. The place was filthy and there were often three to four babies in one crib.

When they met Olivia for the first time, she was underweight and very sick. The people at the orphanage almost did not allow the adoption to go through, as they thought she would be too weak to survive the long plane ride home. But, George and Cindy convinced them that she would receive the best medical care possible when they brought her back to the United States.

Of course, there were a lot of documents to sign and legal paperwork to take care of, but in a couple of days, the three of them would be living as a happy family in Atlanta, Georgia. Michael was just two years old at the time and stayed at home with Olivia's aunt.

Their dream of adopting a little girl was bittersweet. It had taken over a year for the adoption to go through and they were so happy to finally have Olivia. But she was deathly ill, and it would take a miracle for her to recover.

They took Olivia directly from the airport to the emergency room of the local children's hospital. They admitted her to the hospital for several weeks to help her gain weight and get stronger. Then the day finally came when the doctors said that they could take Olivia home.

George had tears in his eyes as he thought about the day that he and his wife walked into their home with their new little baby girl.

CHAPTER 8

"I am sorry Dad," said Olivia as soon as her Dad walked into the office. "I didn't know what else to do with the puppies."

"It's OK," said Dad. He didn't seem mad at all. "I probably would have done the same thing," said Dad as he gave Olivia a big hug.

"Mrs. Clark called Animal Control and they already came to pick up the puppies. They are going to be scared and lonely," Olivia sadly told her Dad.

"I have an idea," said Dad, "How about if we swing by the shelter on the way home and check in on them?"

"Thanks, Dad, that would be great!" Olivia exclaimed.

So, they left the school and were off to the shelter. When they pulled into the parking lot, they could hear lots of barking. The building was run down and there was a terrible odor in the air.

They went to the front desk where an elderly gentleman was sitting. He had a gray mustache and almost no hair on his head. He wore a red plaid shirt and had a nametag that said "Bob – Volunteer."

"How may I help you?" asked Bob.

"We are here to check on some puppies that were brought in about an hour ago. They are really tiny," said Olivia.

"I know exactly the pups that you are referring to…I just put them in a pen together," said Bob.

"I am the one that found them on my way to school this morning. Would you mind if I visit with them for a few minutes?" asked Olivia.

"Sure, follow me," Bob said.

The puppies were so excited to see Olivia. She picked them both up and they gave her kisses all over her face. Their little tails wiggled back and forth, back and forth.

"It is time to go," said Dad. "We will call tomorrow to check on them to make sure they are OK."

On the way out, Olivia asked Bob what would happen to the puppies.

"Well, we hold them for five days to see if someone comes to claim them."

"Then what?" she asked.

"We would put them up for adoption," said Bob.

"For how long?" Olivia asked fearfully.

"If we are full, the animals get up to one week."

Olivia didn't need to ask anything further. She knew what they did to cats and dogs when their time was up.

Chapter 9

Olivia could not stop thinking about the puppies. Every day for the next five days, she called the shelter when she got home from school. The answer was always the same... no one had claimed them.

After the five day holding period, the puppies were given all their shots, had a check-up and were placed in the adoption wing of the building. Olivia hoped and prayed that a nice family would adopt them together.

They had been through so much. They deserved to stay together. After all, they were family.

She continued to call every day to see if they were adopted. She really started to worry when it was close to two weeks and they were still there. Then she received a very devastating phone call. It was from Bob at the shelter.

"I am sorry to have to tell you this, but we are very over crowded right now. If someone doesn't adopt the puppies by 5:00 p.m. tomorrow, they are going to have to be put down."

Olivia couldn't speak. She hung up the phone and started to cry. Then she went to her room, slammed the door and buried herself under the covers. She squeezed her stuffed dog, Sparkles, that she had gotten for Christmas. "How am I going to save the puppies?" she asked Sparkles. She felt so helpless. She wanted so badly to save the puppies and to adopt them. She knew that her parents would never give in because Michael was highly allergic to cats and dogs.

After she cried for almost an hour, Olivia decided to call Madeline and asked her to come over. She had just returned from ballet class and said she would be over as soon as she changed out of her leotard and tights.

The two girls sat on Olivia's bed and decided they needed to come up with a plan. So they went over to Olivia's desk and turned on her laptop. Of course, it was bright pink, her absolute favorite color.

In fact, her entire room was various shades of pink. They began to make a list of ways that they could save the puppies:

1. Take the bus and go get them.

2. Find a home for them on their own by asking kids at school.

3. Beg Olivia's parents to let her keep them.

4. Ask their neighbor to drive them to the shelter and adopt them.

5. Call the shelter and plead with them not to put the puppies down and offer to come after school every day to help care for them.

6. Ask Madeline's parents if they would adopt them.

As they were still trying to think of more solutions, Madeline asked if she ever found out what breed the pups were or how big they would get when they were fully grown. Olivia didn't know a thing about them so they decided to *Google* 'dogs' and see what they could find out. Since the pups were so tiny, they checked small breeds first. They kept scrolling down, looking at dozens and dozens of adorable puppies. Then they both screamed at once…"That's them!"

They were Yorkshire Terriers or "Yorkies" for short. It said that they usually grow to be between three and eight pounds, are very friendly and need to be groomed frequently because they have hair instead of fur. Then the best news ever… most people are <u>NOT</u> allergic to Yorkies.

"Oh my gosh, maybe my parents will let me keep them if it doesn't bother Michael's allergies!" said Olivia.

CHAPTER 10

Olivia ran down the stairs as fast as she could. Madeline followed behind.

"Mom, Dad, I really need to talk to you," said Olivia.

"What is all the commotion?" asked Olivia's Mom.

"The puppies, the Yorkies, non-allergenic!" said Olivia, quickly.

"Slow down Olivia, what are you talking about?" asked her Mom, Cindy.

"I just found out on my computer that the puppies are Yorkshire Terriers and usually do not bother people with dog allergies. Isn't that great news? Can we please adopt them? Please? Please?" begged Olivia.

"Well, we are going to have to talk about this," said her Mother. "We don't want your brother to get sick."

"You only care about Michael because he is your real son! You don't care about me at all! It's not fair! You adopted me when no one else wanted me and now I have a chance to adopt two little puppies that really need me. They are going to be put to sleep if we don't rescue them," she screamed.

Olivia ran up the stairs to her bedroom and once again slammed the door. Madeline decided that it would be best if she went home, as this was a family matter now. She called to Olivia as loud as she could, "see you at school tomorrow, Livy. Bye."

Cindy and George had quite a lengthy discussion about the pups. They knew that their daughter had wanted a dog since she was old enough to speak. On the other hand, they knew their son was highly allergic to animals.

"Maybe we could take the pups on a trial basis," said George. "If Michael is not allergic to them, then we have nothing to lose. If he is, then we will have to find them a new home."

"Let's go up and talk to Olivia."

Chapter 11

"Hey Munchkin." That was one of Dad's nicknames for Olivia, since she was so little. He sometimes even called her "Munchie" for short.

"Your Mom and I just had a discussion about the puppies. We have decided that we will take them on a trial basis to see how Michael does around them."

"Wow! Thanks Mom and Dad. You two are the best!"

"Do not get your hopes up too high," said Mother. "If your brother sneezes or has any difficulty breathing at all, we will have to find them another loving home. Is it a deal Olivia?"

"Yes, Mom. Thanks so much."

"Can we go right now and get them? It's only 5:30 and they are open until 6:00 p.m. PLEASE, PLEASE?" asked Olivia.

"Ok, but go get your brother," said Mom.

"Can Madeline come with us too?"

"Sure, she can."

"I will call her and tell her we will pick her up on the way."

So they all climbed in their car and were off to get the puppies. Olivia was so excited that she could hardly sit still.

CHAPTER 12

Even though the shelter was less than ten miles from their house, it seemed like it took hours to get there. Dad barely had a chance to put the car in park, when Olivia jumped out of the back seat and ran through the front entrance of the shelter. "Wait for me!" yelled Madeline. She did not even check in at the front desk and ran as fast as her little legs could go, directly to the puppy area. Her heart sank when she went to the pen where the little puppies were once kept. "Oh my gosh! They are gone!" Olivia's heart sunk.

Olivia ran to her Mom and told her the puppies were gone. She began to cry uncontrollably. Mom hugged her tight, but Olivia could not be consoled.

They all went to the front desk where Bob was sitting. "I tried to warn you Olivia, but you ran past so quickly. You are about 20 minutes too late. A rescue group just came and picked them up. Don't worry, they are safe now. *Angels Among Us Pet Rescue* is a wonderful group and they will find a loving home for the puppies. They require an adoption application, a meet and greet, a vet check, and even do a home visit."

Olivia wiped away her tears but could hardly speak. "I, I know, but

I wanted to adopt the puppies. I wanted to be their mother and take care of them forever. I even had names picked out for them… They are so tiny. I was going to call them Itsy and Bitsy."

"Mr. Bob, could you please give us the phone number of *Angels Among Us*?" Dad asked.

"I don't have a number but can give you their website," Bob replied. "They will list the pups on Petfinder as soon as they take them to the vet for a check up to make sure they are healthy. Then the pups will go to a special foster home for two weeks, just to be sure they don't come down with Parvo or other puppy diseases. After that, the puppies will be available for adoption!"

The Preston family and Madeline all got back in the car to head home. "Anyone for ice cream?" said Dad. "No thanks," said Olivia, still sniffling and trying to hold back the tears. So they dropped Madeline off at her house and Olivia went straight to her room when they got home. She opened up her pink computer and logged in. She typed in the website for *Angels Among Us Pet Rescue* (AAU) that Mr. Bob had given her. The puppies were not yet listed on Petfinder, as it had only been a little over an hour since they had picked up the pups.

She did, however, see a place where she could leave a comment. She started out by typing, "My name is Olivia Preston…" and briefly told her story about Itsy and Bitsy and asked them to please get in touch with her as soon as possible. She even left her phone number.

She closed her computer and snuggled in bed with Sparkles. "I need those puppies, and the puppies need me!" she said to Sparkles. "My Mom and Dad came for me and adopted me when no one else wanted me. Now I want to adopt Itsy and Bitsy so they can know what it feels like to be loved." Olivia finally cried herself to sleep.

Later that night, the phone rang. Dad answered, "Yes, this is the Preston residence. Yes, I have a daughter named Olivia. Just a minute please, and I will get her." Olivia picked up the phone. "Hi Olivia, my name is Miss Lisa and I am with *Angels Among Us*. I just read your message and wanted to call you to tell you that the puppies are safe and healthy. We took them for a complete checkup at one of our top veterinarian clinics in the area. Dr. Becky and Dr. Diana checked them out and they are happy, healthy and strong, thanks to you!"

"Could you have your Mom or Dad help you fill out the adoption application? You can fill it out online. One of our Angels will review it and get back to you within a couple of days."

"Thank you so much! We will fill it out right away," said Olivia. "Olivia, you did a very kind act saving those little puppies. We at *Angels Among Us* thank you so much and are so proud of you!" said the kind woman on the phone.

As soon as Olivia got off the phone, she asked her parents if they would fill out the application. The three of them sat at the kitchen table and answered the questions on the form together. When it was completed, Olivia asked if she could press "submit." And so she did and the waiting began, again...

CHAPTER 13

The next day, Olivia and Madeline ran home from the bus stop. To their surprise, Itsy and Bitsy were in a little puppy pen on the kitchen floor. Olivia screamed with joy, "Mom, Dad, what is going on? Mom, what are you doing home so early?"

"Well, honey, I know how important this adoption is to you and I wanted to be here to share in your joy and excitement!"

"That's so cool, Mom. Thanks for coming home early! I love you so much!"

"Itsy and Bitsy are officially your puppies! A volunteer from *Angels Among Us* reviewed our application, and came over to see our house while you were at school," Dad explained. "Everything checked out fine, so I signed the adoption agreement and paid the adoption fee. They usually require dogs to be in a foster home for two weeks before they can be adopted, but under the circumstances and since we don't have any other pets, they agreed to go ahead with the adoption. We cannot take them to pet stores or dog parks for several weeks so they won't catch any diseases. Also, don't forget about our original agreement. We have to make sure that Michael doesn't have an allergic reaction to them."

"I know Dad. Thank you so much! I love you!"

Dad stayed home to keep an eye on Itsy and Bitsy, while Mom, Olivia, Michael and Madeline headed to the pet supply store. Of course, Olivia picked out everything in pink. Water bowl, food bowls, leashes, and collars, all pink. They also got some cute toys, food, treats, and of course, ID tags labeled with the puppies' names and the Preston's phone number.

When they returned home, all three kids climbed in the puppy pen and began playing with Itsy and Bitsy. They fed them and gave them cold water. The pups were very playful and kept giving puppy kisses.

This was the happiest Olivia had been in weeks.

After the puppies finally fell asleep, the family ordered a pepperoni pizza to celebrate. Madeline went home after dinner, so everyone could do their homework. Olivia was still so excited that she could hardly focus on the math problems in front of her. She was on the floor next to her very own pups, doing her homework.

Chapter 14

The next morning, Olivia woke up in her sleeping bag on the kitchen floor. Mom and Dad let her sleep there just this once, so the puppies wouldn't be scared. After she fed Itsy and Bitsy and gave them each a kiss, she went upstairs to see if Michael was awake. She gave him a nudge, as he was still fast asleep. "How are you feeling, Michael?"

"I was doing just fine until you woke me up," Michael said sleepily.

"I'm serious, are you having any trouble breathing?" asked Olivia.

"I'm fine, now will you let me get back to sleep? It's only 4:30 in the morning!"

"Ok, I'm sorry, I didn't know it was that early."

Olivia went back downstairs, but this time she put her sleeping bag inside the puppy pen. Itsy and Bitsy climbed right in and snuggled tight with their new mommy. "I will take care of you forever and ever. You will never have to be scared, cold, or hungry again. I love you both so much."

Angels Among Us Pet Rescue is a 501(c)(3) non-profit charity operating through the assistance of a network of volunteers who have a love for animals and a desire to save dogs and cats from high kill shelters.

Our mission is to educate the general public about the plight of animals stuck in shelters, and to see these rescued souls down a pathway from possible death, to being rescued, vetted, repaired and fostered, then through transition into a loving forever home with a family to care for them the rest of their journey.

Through our Angels Youth Ambassadors program, we educate our younger generation about humanely caring for animals, and encourage all pet owners to spay and neuter their pets to help control the unwanted pet population.

Please visit our website at *www.angelsrescue.org* for additional information about Angels Rescue - our mission, goals and successes. To view our adoptable pets in need of "forever" homes, please visit our website at *www.angelsrescue.org/adopt*. You may also contact us by email at *Info@angelsrescue.org*.

A portion of the proceeds of this book will go to Angels Among Us Pet Rescue.

If you are considering adding a new furry member to your family, please visit your local shelter or a rescue group such as Angels Among us. Save a life... Adopt, don't shop.

ABOUT THE AUTHOR

Peggy Rydberg was born on Long Island, New York. She earned her Bachelor of Science degree in Education at Keene State College in New Hampshire and her Master's degree in Early Childhood Education at Oglethorpe University in Atlanta, Georgia. She is a former school teacher and has taught pre-school, kindergarten, second and third grade. She now is a figure skating coach and pet sitter.

Miss Rydberg currently lives in Marietta, GA with her four beloved dogs, Millie, Holly, Kalli and Tasha.

She is actively involved with animal rescue and *Angels Among Us* and has fostered over two hundred dogs and puppies with various rescue groups.

CPSIA information can be obtained at www.ICGtesting.com
Printed in the USA
LVOW04s0523290515

440317LV00001B/2/P